Teaching Poetry with 7–12 year olds

Teaching Poetry with 7–12 year olds

Alan Peat

IM IMAGINATIVE MINDS

Imaginative Minds Limited
Birmingham
2008

Imaginative MInds Limited
215 The Green House, Gibb Street, Birmingham B9 4AA

First published in 2000

ISBN: 9781904806479

Cover design, text design and illustration by Al Stewart

Printed in the UK

Acknowledgements

My thanks to Sam Larkham Dever for recommending me, and to Mike Venet for suggesting that I write this.

'Busy Day', by Michael Rosen, from *You Tell Me*, by Roger McGough and Michael Rosen (Kestrel 1979), copyright © Michael Rosen, 1979, is reproduced by permission of Penguin Books Ltd.

'You'd Better Beware' and 'Fishy Tale', poems and illustrations by Colin McNaughton, from *There's an Awful Lot of Weirdos in our Neighbourhood* by Colin McNaughton, Walker Books 1990, copyright © Colin McNaughton, 1987/1990, are reproduced by permission of Colin McNaughton and Walker Books Ltd.

Contents

For
Hannah Petch and Michael Peat
from Uncle Alan

Introduction

Poetry should be a stimulating aspect of literacy teaching although it is often the 'Cinderella' of literacy and as such 'plays third fiddle' to fiction and non-fiction writing. Poetry should not take third place in the pantheon of literacy but rather should be treated on equal terms with both story writing and non fiction. For many reluctant writers the 'constraints' of poetry paradoxically offer a 'safety net' which helps to build self confidence.

As a teaching aid, this book has been designed to save classroom teachers' valuable time by explicitly linking each poem to one or more explicit objective. A 'Notes for Teachers' section accompanies each poem and includes both suggestions for using the poem with either a whole class or group, and extension activities.

The poems can be used in a shared writing context as

(a) models for collaborative writing
(b) starting points for extension work
(c) subjects for comment/evaluation/discussion

The poems have been selected on a basis of 'pupil response'. Children are the keenest of critics and as a performance poet visiting schools during book weeks I have had the opportunity to 'road test' all of the poems which are included. The enjoyment factor has therefore been at the heart of the selection process.

The writer Eavan Boland compared poetry to mining: 'One day you strike, and strike the rock and nothing happens; the next, you hit it, and extract silver.' It is the author's hope that the poems and ideas in this slim volume will help more pupils to "extract the silver" from the bedrock of language.

If we foster a lifelong love of poetry then we need to explicitly share our enjoyment of poems with our pupils. The 'I really like this one because......' approach is a powerful model to use in the classroom.

The final selection of poems for this book was based on the precept that if you can meet clear teaching objectives using materials which create a sense of fun, then you can foster the idea that poetry and enjoyment are intrinsically linked. This, surely, is a useful first step on the road to ensuring that our pupils are willing 'word miners'!

How to use this book

With ease of access in mind, this collection begins with simple objectives which increase in complexity throughout the book.

In the 'Teachers' Notes' section, which accompanies each poem, suggestions for both rhyming and non-rhyming poems are included. Many of the exemplar poems have a distinct rhyme scheme as they were written for performance. It is hoped, however, that teachers will stress that rhyme is only one tool in the poet's armoury. For this reason, non-rhyming forms such as haiku, tanka, expanding and contracting poems and concrete poems are included in the notes.

Responding to poems: writing frames for poetry

Maureen Lewis and David Wray have undertaken much excellent work in relation to helping children both respond to non-fiction texts and to write in a range of non-fiction genres. Writing frames to guide and scaffold written work (a key feature of the EXCEL project, Wray and Lewis 1997) can be adapted to help pupils to respond more effectively to poetry.

The following 'writing frames for poetry' can be very useful in allowing the teacher to model a response to a poem (or poems) and explicitly discuss features of response. They also provide the pupils with a coherent structural framework for responding to poetry which does not constrain the content, but rather help to guide the pupil toward a coherent finished piece of writing. The sentence-starters assist the children to produce pieces that are well structured.

The 'Can you use?' boxes can contain subject-specific vocabulary prompts or more general vocabulary such as a variety of connectives. The teacher can use this part of the frame to guide pupils away from an over-reliance on 'and then'. The content can also be varied according to the individual needs of pupils.

The frames are photocopiable within the institution of purchase but a 'death by worksheet' model of usage should be avoided at all costs! When using the frames try to aim for working toward weaning the pupils off them. The frames are a means of structuring independence and this aim should be shared with the pupils before they are used. To encourage extended writing, it may be useful to enlarge the frames to an A3 format.

There are clear and incontrovertible benefits to be gained from familiarising pupils with (and encouraging the use of) the language of poetry; to be able to discuss a poem using the meta-language of poetry – onomatopoeia, metaphor, couplet, simile, and so on. One of the best methods of learning is through doing: the pupil who can use a metaphor in their own writing will be able to talk about metaphors in the work of other poets far better than a pupil who has merely been told what a metaphor is. The language of poetry can be filtered through the writing frames which follow. They should, however, be used to embed and reinforce understanding rather than as an end in themselves.

FRAME 1

Responding to a single poem (describing likes and dislikes)

This frame includes a challenge to use the word 'because' five or more times. This encourages pupils to justify, rather than merely state, their likes and dislikes. The frame includes elements of enumeration (First... Secondly) and can easily be adapted so that the focus of any writing is an aspect of the poem, such as 'use of language'. Additional text boxes can be added for further challenge, e.g. 'The penultimate feature I wish to consider is...'.

FRAME 2

Responding to two poems (contrast frame)

The poems in this collection can be grouped so that pupils are encouraged to respond critically and state preferences. This frame concentrates on the language of contrast, assisting pupils to write about two dissimilar poems.

For this purpose, a useful twinning is: *A Slithering Poem* (visual non-rhymed concrete poem) and *You'd Better Beware (A Reptile Rap)* (rhyming couplets, six-line stanzas).

FRAME 3

Responding to two poems (comparison frame)

A number of the poems in this collection lend themselves to pairing due to similar features such as the use of rhyming couplets and humour. It is also profitable to apply a comparison frame to two poems which are apparently dissimilar. This use of the frame facilitates a higher cognitive demand level and encourages a close scrutiny of the poems.

FRAME 4

Comparison and contrast grid

This frame functions as a graphic organiser for comparing and contrasting two poems. The concept could easily be extended so that pupils are comparing and contrasting three or more poems, thereby differentiating usage for varying ability levels whilst focusing on the same objective. This application of different tiers of challenge represents an effective way to personalise use of the frames with individual children.

FRAME 5

Frame to persuade a friend that the poem is good!

The language of persuasion surrounds us and it is important that pupils are proficient in their use of persuasive language. This frame links this non-fiction genre to a poetic starting point.

Name	**Date**

Title

The first reason why I like/dislike the poem is

Secondly I like/dislike

An additional feature I like/dislike is

Furthermore

Finally

Can you use?
Can you use the word 'because' five or more times in your writing?

Frame 1 *Responding to a single poem (describing likes and dislikes)*

Frame 2 *Responding to two poems (contrast frame)*

Name	**Date**

Title

.... and .... are different in many ways. The most obvious difference is

A further feature which is dissimilar is

They are unlike in their use of

They also contrast in their use of

These are not the only differences: another is

Finally

Can you use?

whilst

Frame 3 *Responding to two poems (comparison frame)*

Name	**Date**

Title

Although................................and ....
are different, they also have similar features. Firstly,

Secondly, they are both

They are alike in their use of

There are further similarities such as

Additionally

Furthermore

Finally

Can you use?

Frame 4 *Comparison and contrast grid*

Name		**Date**
Title		
Features	***Poem 1*** *Title.....................*	***Poem 2*** *Title.....................*
Form (such as haiku, rap etc.)		
Free verse or rhyme?		
Onomatopoeia		
Simile?		
Metaphor?		

Frame 4 *Comparison and contrast grid*

Name	**Date**
Title	

Features	***Poem 1*** *Title......................*	***Poem 2*** *Title......................*
Exciting features?		
Serious or humorous?		
Age range aimed at?		
Interesting words		

Frame 5 *Frame to persuade a friend that the poem is worth reading!*

Name	**Date**
Poem chosen	**Poet**

Although not everyone would agree, I think.............................. is an excellent poem because

My second reason for recommending it is

A further reason is

Furthermore

I believe that the most exciting thing about the poem is

Therefore, although some people might argue that other poems are better, I think I have demonstrated that

Can you use?

Teaching Poetry with 7–12 year olds

Poems and Teachers' Notes

poem

Animal Party

(An A-Z poem with a mysterious missing letter!)

Albert the Aardvark only ate ants,
Bertie the Beaver gnawed bushes and plants,
Colin the Chameleon was changing his colour,
Douglas the Dalmatian came along with his mother,
Edward the Elephant only ate eggs,
Freddy the Ferret brought beer in a keg,
Greta the Gerbil ate the bulk of the meal
While Harold the Hippo fell head over heels
With Irene Iguana who basked in the sun,
You can tell that the party was really quite fun.

Jasper the Jay was scoffing the jelly,
Kate Kangaroo sat there watching the telly,
Lucinda the Llama was eating ice cream,
Matilda the Minnow could hardly be seen,
Nosey the Newt knew everyone's news,
Oliver Orang-utan polished his shoes,
Peter the Python was hissing a tune,
Quentin the Quail just stared up at the moon,
Ronald the Rat was admiring his tail,
Sammy the Slug left a bright silver trail.

Tina the Tuna fish splashed in the sink,
Ursula Unicorn finished her drink,
Vera the Vole burrowed under the floor,
Wilbert the Walrus was stood by the door,
Xanthippus the X-Ray fish showed off his bones,
Zoey the Zebra refused to go home,
And the only creature who did not show,
Despite being asked if he wanted to go
Was Desmond the Dodo whose reply was succinct,
'I cannot turn up as you see I'm extinct!'

Animal Party

An ideal poem to use with seven to ten year olds when concentrating on creating patterns with words.

Activity one: Replacements

After reading and discussing the form of the poem, establish what the missing letter is, then explain to the class/group that they will be returning to this in order to write their own alphabet poem with a missing letter.

Choose an 'easy' letter such as 'A' and write this on a large sheet of paper. Now invite suggestions for both animals and names which begin with that letter, e.g. replace Albert with Andrew in line one. This could result in suggestions such as Anne, Aziz, Adrian etc. and antelope, ant, anteater etc.

Now brainstorm things that can be eaten other than ants, e.g. apples, apricots, anchovies etc. Finally, create several new first lines using new names, animals and foodstuffs, e.g. Anne the antelope always ate apricots.

Activity two: Extensions

Explain to the class/group that the new first line they have created is going to be extended. This could be achieved by adding a range of embedded clauses to the first line, e.g. Anne the antelope, *who lived in Africa,* always ate apricots.

Return to the original poem and see if the class/group can add extensions to other lines of the poem in the same way, e.g. Bertie the Beaver, who lived in a boat, gnawed bushes and plants.

(NB Accept suggestions which are grammatically correct and don't worry too much about the literal!)

A resource such as Mike Wilks' *Ultimate Alphabet* (Pavilion Books) is a useful starting point as there are many objects hidden within the single page illustrations which relate to each letter of the alphabet. As these often number several hundreds, the book is invaluable for pupils who are 'stuck'!

Finally, consider utilising pre-questioning technique prior to reading the poem in order to lend a focus to the pupils' listening. Two useful questions to ask are:

1 Can you tell me the name of the creature which is mythical?
2 Can you tell me the name of the creature which is extinct?

Answers should only be provided after listening to the poem.

Key Objective:

To collect suitable words and phrases, in order to write poems and short descriptions; design simple patterns with words.

Teachers' notes

A Slithering Poem

S
na
ke,
snake
slithers,
poison
fanged,
through
grass,
scaly
body
over
earth,
under
leaves,
bright
pattern,
forked
tongue
flickering
sliding
gliding,
cold
blooded
mouth
opening
wider,
wider,
snake
bites
then
slides
and
hisses,
snake
sna
ke
s
n
a
k e

A Slithering Poem

A Slithering Poem is an example of a 'shape poem', or more accurately a 'concrete poem', so called because it sets in the shape of the thing which is being written about. When choosing a thin object as the theme of a concrete poem I usually focus on verbs, as is the case in *A Slithering Poem*.

If the poem is being handwritten, it is best to start by asking the pupils to draw a faint outline of their chosen subject. This is then 'filled in' with the poem itself. Concrete poems are an excellent form for producing on the computer as time can be spent reducing and expanding fonts as well as in using the return key, tab key and space bar.

If, for example, a bottle was chosen as a subject, pupils could use a smaller font when 'filling in' the neck of the bottle and could expand the size of the font when completing the main body of the bottle.

The opportunity to combine literacy and information technology should not be missed when working on this form.

Key Objective:

To invent calligrams and a range of shape poems, selecting appropriate words and careful presentation. Build up class collections.

Once upon . . .

Once upon a sugar mountain way up in the sky,
Once upon a tennis bat, once upon a fly,
Once upon a bag of sweets, once upon a spoon,
Once upon a lump of cheese, once upon the moon,
Once upon a ticking clock, once upon an hour,
Once upon a puff of smoke, once upon a flower,
Once upon a pond of frogs, once upon a bat,
Once upon a story and it started just like that!

Once upon...

Once upon... is a list poem. There are numerous ways of producing list poems which are enjoyable to write. A favourite with 7-12 year olds is the 'Becoming more ridiculous/ludicrous' method. A suitable phrase to start each line is chosen such as 'I forgot my homework because...' A list poem is then developed in which the ideas are at first sensible, e.g. 'I forgot my homework because I had to make breakfast this morning'. As the list poem progresses, the ideas must *gradually* become more ridiculous (less believable) so that the poem could end with: 'I forgot my homework because a giant alien spaceship landed in my garden this morning and startled me'.

Other useful starting phrases include, 'I didn't go to school because...'/ 'I stayed in bed because...'/ 'Yesterday I...'

A way to develop the example included in this collection is to introduce neologisms. A neologism is a newly-coined word – one that has just been invented. Begin by explaining that you have invented a word: 'Brumbazi'.

Ask the class/group to suggest what this word might mean and then offer them your definition, e.g.

> Brumbazi, *n.* a musical instrument played with the ear.

(This provides a useful opportunity to discuss how a dictionary is 'laid out', particularly using *n. vb. adj.* and *pl.* (plural)).

Next, assign clusters of letters (A-E, F-L etc.) to various groups of pupils and begin to write your 'Dictionary of Neologisms'.

These can then be used in a list poem of choice, applying the rule that each line should 'make sense', e.g. if the dictionary included the word and definition,

> Pipplepopple, *n.* a very hairy goat that smells like chocolate,

the line of a 'Once upon...' list poem which includes it could read –

> 'Once upon a time I was running through a field when I saw a Pipplepopple'.

You should also model and discuss lines that *don't* work and explain why.

Key Objectives:

a) To collect suitable words and phrases, in order to write poems and short descriptions; design simple patterns with words.

b) To experiment with language, e.g. creating new words, similes and metaphors.

poem

The Big Race (A single letter poem)

There's a rapid rushing rabbit
Running round the racing track
With a rattlesnake behind him
And a raven on his back,
And the reindeer's been disqualified
For wearing roller-skates
And the reptile didn't even start
As he arrived too late.

They round the bend,
They raise some dust,
The crowd's roar raises rafters,
A raccoon trips upon a rock,
A reed frog falls soon after,
A robin flies above the race,
A rook brings up the rear,
In a rising cloud of dust a rhino disappears.

They reach the final stretch of track,
The rabbit wins the gold,
The rhino comes in second
But he blames it on his cold.

The Big Race

The Big Race is a poem based around a single letter of the alphabet – in this case the letter 'R'. To ensure that the pupils are attentive, I play a competitive game ('Beat the Peat'). I explain that there are many words beginning with the letter R in the poem which I am about to read, and that the pupils will have to name seven at the end of the poem. I then explain that there is also a rule that if they repeat someone else's suggestion then I win the point back.This ensures that they are listening to each other as well as the teacher!

When this process is complete another letter of the alphabet is chosen, after which the class brainstorms words beginning with this letter which can be used in the final poem.

It is possible to differentiate this activity by giving groups of different abilities specific tasks such as:

> Nouns beginning with…
> Verbs beginning with…
> Adjectives beginning with…
> Adverbs beginning with…
> etc.

To this we could add themes, e.g. 'Animals beginning with…' Written large, these are then 'posted up' around the class to form a stimulus for the pupils' own single letter poems.

The Big Race can also be used to reinforce the concept of alliteration in poetry (the use of the same consonant or vowel repeatedly in a line of verse.)

I use the tongue-twister 'Around the rugged rock the ragged rascal ran' as a further starting point and play the language game 'alliterative sentences'. For this the class/group has to suggest three themes, e.g. sport/fashion/music, after which alliterative sentences are produced:

> Sport: Football fans think football is fantastic.
>
> Fashion: She wore a dress that looked divine with diamonds on her digits!

Note that not every word need begin with the chosen letter, just the majority. I find it preferable to limit the number of names used in an alliterative sentence to one so that we avoid sentences like:

> Sport: Sam, Samantha, Stan and Sylvia play soccer with Simon and Saul.

Key Objectives:

a) To write new or extended verses for 'performance' and oral poetry read, e.g. rhythms, repetition.

b) To write poetry that uses sound to create effects, e.g. onomatopoeia, *alliteration*, distinctive rhythms.

Teachers' notes

poem

Busy Day

Michael Rosen

Pop in
pop out
pop over the road
pop out for a walk
pop in for a talk
pop down to the shop
can't stop
got to pop

got to pop?

pop where?
pop what?

well
I've got to
pop round
pop up
pop in to town
pop out and see
pop in for tea
pop down to the shop
can't stop
got to pop

got to pop?

pop where?
pop what?

well
I've got to
pop in
pop out
pop over the road
pop out for a walk
pop in for a talk . . . .

Busy Day (Michael Rosen)

Michael Rosen's *Busy Day* is an ideal poem to use as a starting point when exploring poetry which uses sound to create effects. After reading the poem, pupils choose an onomatopoeic word (a word whose sound is imitative of the noise an object makes). If they are unfamiliar with onomatopoeia, begin by asking them to tell you what sound a hammer makes ('clang' etc.). They could then make suggestions for words which convey the sound of other everyday objects (brush – swish/ toaster – pop, etc.). When they have chosen their word they then have to think of as many things that could make that sound as possible and draft a list, e.g. if they chose 'plop' (a popular choice!) then the list might begin:

> A stone being dropped in water
> A frog jumping off a lily pad
> A bucket at the bottom of a well

If they find it difficult to produce a long list, encourage unusual ideas by modelling some:

> A Martian sinking its tentacle into some slime
> A man jumping into a pool of custard, etc.

The pupils then work on a finished poem by reordering their lines, adding the onomatopoeic word either at the end or the start of each line. (This presents the teacher with a useful opportunity to discuss end-of-line, and initial, rhyme.)

A further child-friendly way of introducing onomatopoeia is through the use of video excerpts taken from the popular 1960s *Batman* series ('Pow!'/'Sock!' etc!)

By way of an extension activity, pupils can write a poem which tells a story, with the added rule that it should contain a repeating onomatopoeic word. The following example can be used as a model:

> There's a train on the clickety-clack track
> Taking clickety-clack people
> To clickety-clack places.
> See them eat their clickety snacks,
> Pre-packed and plastic wrapped.
> There's Uncle Jim and his friend Jack,
> The whole wide world's on the clickety clack
> Old, young, sad and happy
> Clickety click clack, clickety-clackety.

The book *The Story of the Little Mole who knew it was None of his Business* by Werner Holzwarth (ISBN 1856 0210 17) is, without doubt, one of the best resources for making the concept stick!

Key Objective:

To write poetry that uses sound to create effects, e.g. *onomatopoeia*, alliteration, distinctive rhythms.

poem

Cliff

It was really unexpected, it was somewhat of a shock
When my brother, who was aged just five, turned into a rock.
We wanted to include him, brothers shouldn't be left out,
So we put him in a wheelbarrow and pushed the lad about.
We pushed him to a disco but his dancing skills were weak,
We wanted him to talk to girls but found he couldn't speak,
Then people started joking and they never seemed to stop,
'Say, is that your brother? He's a real chip off the block.'
And I think they thought it funny but I knew he was alone,
It really cannot be much fun to be a lump of stone.

And so the years flew by at speed and he and I grew older,
My brother who was once a rock, soon became a boulder,
'Little Mike' seemed rather odd and so we changed his name
but somehow shouting out 'Hey Cliff' just didn't seem the same.
The barrow's wheels buckled and we had to buy a truck,
But our Cliff's days were numbered, he was almost out of luck.
We turned a corner sharply and he rolled off down the lane
With little pieces breaking off, he'd never look the same...
Suddenly he struck a wall, there was a mighty CRASH
And poor Cliff ended off his days as bags of pebbledash.

Cliff

Cliff is based on the premise that a person can turn to stone and as such falls well within the sphere of 'imagined experience'. In workshops I discuss the ways in which a writer can make the most extraordinary event seem believable. Having a person turn to stone is not in itself plausible, yet the accumulation of small details thereafter renders it credible. When writing poems based on 'imagined experience', I tend to stress the idea of accumulating small details.

Useful starting points for poems written by pupils include:

(a) The day my belly turned to jelly
(b) When I became water!
(c) Becoming an insect I have just tried to swat

All of these ideas demand an empathetic response from the writer – the ability to put oneself into another person/thing's situation and to assume the feelings which they/it might have.

When developing poems directly from *Cliff*, I stress that in my poem the boy turns to stone. I then explain that we are going to write poems in which a person becomes something else (other than stone!). We then begin by answering the following two questions:

1 What will the person in my poem turn into?
2 What will they become at the end of their days?*

*Note that in *Cliff* the boy ends off his days as 'bags of pebbledash'. This is related to stone – it is something which stone could logically become. Therefore if the pupils choose 'sand' as an answer to question one, a logical thing which they could become at the end of their days would be a sandcastle. Likewise, if they chose 'a teapot' in answer to question one, then 'broken pieces of pottery' would be a sensible answer to question two.

By answering these two questions, the start and end of the poem are defined and, therefore, the main body of the poem will deal with how the teapot is broken or how the sand becomes a sandcastle, etc. There is also an opportunity to discuss alliteration by focusing on the line:

'The *b*arrow's wheels *b*uckled and we had to *b*uy a truck.'

Key Objective:

To write poems based on personal or *imagined* experience, linked to poems read.

poem

The Dandy Lion

Oh, you really must meet the dandy lion,
All the other beasts were crying,
A black bow tie and a pair of spats,
He really knows where it is at.

Cufflinks and a fine starched collar,
He sets the trends, he doesn't follow,
His monacle's clasped tight to his eye,
He really is a dandy guy.

Imagination, flair and wit,
He really is a dandy hit.
Charm and grace and poise and style,
You'll really love his dandy smile!

How I relished our first meeting,
Dreamed about the dandy greeting,
Hand in paw we'd shake and bow
And all the beasts would cry out *Wow!*

But at the end of my long search,
I found him growing in the dirt,
Things were not as I'd assumed
Although he looked fine in full bloom.

He had no teeth, he had no roar,
He had no mane, he had no paw,
He had no growl, no beastly power,
To my surprise I'd found a flower!

The Dandy Lion

The poem functions as a pun on the word dandelion and makes use of the archaic word 'dandy' meaning 'very fine'. It's worth pointing out to the class/group that when used as a noun, a dandy is a man who is greatly concerned with his personal appearance, particularly his clothing. One of the most noted dandies was George Bryan Brummell (1778-1840), known as 'Beau' Brummell because of his dandyism. The poem makes reference to this meaning of the word when describing clothing of the past.

Activities

(a) How many items of clothing and accessories can the class/group name which are 'archaic'?
(b) Using an assortment of books, can the class/group produce an A–Z of clothing/fashion for a given historical period? (This activity provides you with an opportunity to reinforce crucial information–retrieval skills).
(c) Pupils can then produce their own poems using archaic words, using a similar rhyme form to the example given.

Teaching points: draw attention to the near-rhymes in the first two stanzas, i.e. lion/crying, collar/follow. (You could also consider producing near-rhymes for words on the pupils' A–Z list.)

It is a good idea to teach the pupils how to record a rhyme scheme. For example, a poem in which the first two lines rhyme (a couplet) and are then followed by a further couplet (which does not rhyme with the first two lines) would have a rhyme scheme of:

a a b b

If, however, the rhyming words were *identical* in the first two lines, the rhyme scheme would be:

A A b b

Key Objective:

To write poetry based on the structure and/or style of poems read, e.g. taking account of *vocabulary, archaic expressions, patterns of rhyme, choruses, similes.*

Teachers' notes

poem

Swimming Trunks Disaster

It was the kind of day, you know, that would be best forgot,
My trunk elastic swinging loose, I hadn't tied the knot,
My friends were dressed in lycra but my swimming trunks were baggy,
And when the water touched them they just swelled up then went
saggy.

I doggy-paddled awkwardly and really felt a fool,
My red-rimmed eyes were closing (chlorine-damaged from the pool!)
And then the girl I fancied walked in looking kind of sweet,
She'd never fall for baggy trunks, they really were not neat.

I'd tried to grow some muscles for her, cut down on my chips,
I longed to kiss her on the cheek and maybe (once) the lips!
I needed her attention, make her know I was alive,
There was only one thing for it, I would have to do *THE DIVE!*

I stepped up to the low board and simply shook my head,
Walked up to the second one, looked down, thought 'I'm dead',
Crawled up to the top one, I was shivering and quaking,
Thinking 'What an awful noise my teeth right now are making.'

And just then she looked up at me, I simply tossed my hair,
Then raising arms up heavenward I dived into the air…
My trunks were wrapped around my feet and then they blew right off,
I swam around with nothing on and soon began to cough.

A lifeguard brought them back to me with everybody staring,
There's nothing more embarrassing than trunkless bottom-baring,
Wearing them was dreadful, like some horrendous curse,
But falling nude from top boards is really rather worse!!!

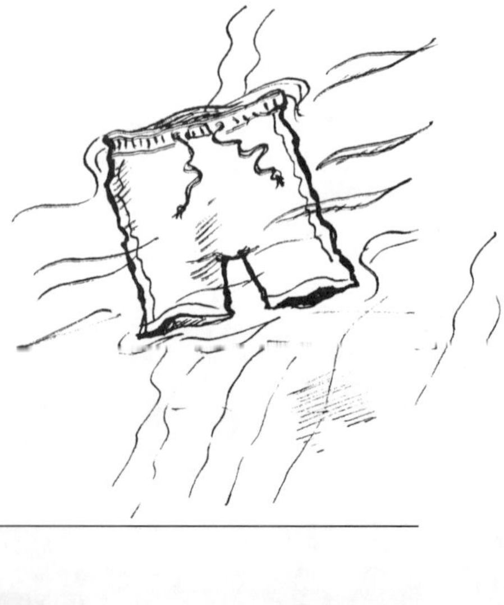

Swimming Trunks Disaster

When reading this poem to pupils I often refer to a phrase which the poet Gary Boswell uses: 'think weird!'. Basically, this involves the pupils in transforming an everyday event into a *think weird* event. To do this, model the process with one or two examples on a writing surface which can be seen clearly by the class/group, and then invite the pupils to continue with suggestions for the two columns:

Everyday event	***Think weird* event**
1 Go to swimming baths	1 Swimming trunks fall off
2 Brush teeth	2 Toothbrush gets stuck up nose
3 Take dog for a walk	3 Dog begins to speak

If the concept of an 'everyday' event gets lost in the excitement which this process inevitably generates, then replace 'everyday' with 'dull/boring'.The pupils then select an everday event and related 'think weird' event from the list and begin their poem. As an extra input you could discuss rhyming couplets and suggest this as a structure for their poem.

Three methods of differentiating this activity are:

(a) *Bout-rimés* were popular in the eighteenth century and by the nineteenth century filling in the lines of poetry to prepared rhymes had become a fashionable parlour game. In a class situation the teacher provides the end-of-line rhyming words and the pupils have to build a poem around these, e.g.

______________________________ day
______________________________ pay
______________________________ do
______________________________ you etc.

Bout-rimés can be most useful for pupils who are beginning to use rhyme but are unsure of the layout of end-of-line rhyme.

(b) More complex still is *initial rhyme*, i.e. where the words at the start of each line are used to form the rhyme, e.g.

Day by day I earn more money
Pay me now and make me happy
Do you like to win some cash?
You do and guess what? So do I!

(c) One further variant on this theme is 'eye rhyme' in which couplets look as if they will rhyme, e.g. bough/cough. When the couplets are read aloud, however, they do not truly rhyme. Pupils can be asked to find other examples and use these in their own poems.

Key Objective:

To write poetry based on the structure and/or style of poems read, e.g. taking account of vocabulary, archaic expressions, *patterns of rhyme*, choruses, similes.

poem

Epitaph for Len

Here lies luckless liar Len,
A giant among lying men,
We thought death would stop him but to our surprise
Six feet under Len still lies.

Epitaph for Len

An epitaph is a commemorative inscription designed for either a tombstone or a monument. The example included was chosen because of the additional use of the final pun on the word 'lies'.

Pupils can use the four-line a/a/b/b rhyme scheme as a structural template for their own epitaphs. It is productive to combine this with historical research into the Victorians so that the pupils write epitaphs for people in professions that are no longer common, such as blacksmith, wheelwright, lamplighter, etc.

Extension activities include the production of both acrostics and telestichs for a range of professions. The acrostic is frequently used in primary classrooms, though usage of the telestich is less common. An example of each form, which can be used as a model with the pupils, is given here. In an acrostic the 'theme-word' is spelled vertically at the start of each line whereas in a telestich the theme-word is spelled vertically at the end of the line.

Acrostic
*D*octors help you when you're feeling ill
*O*lder people often get illnesses that require a doctor
*C*olds and 'flu are treated by them
*T*hermometers are used by doctors to take our temperature
*O*pen-heart surgery is performed by doctors
*R*elaxing is something doctors aren't familiar with!

Telestich
We called for a doctor when I felt ba*d*
He asked if I was feeling O.K.; I replied 'N*o*'
I said 'What can you do to help me do*c*?'
Well, he took my temperature and said he'd never seen such hea*t*
Then he gave me some medicine and murmured that he had to g*o*
He ran off then but I'll never forget how quickly I felt bette*r*.

A variation is the hidden acrostic, i.e. the theme word can be hidden anywhere within the lines such as in the first letter of the second word of each line or the third letter of each line, etc.

Key Objective:

To write poetry based on the structure and/or style of poems read, e.g. taking account of vocabulary, archaic expressions, patterns of rhyme, choruses, similes.

Teachers' notes

poem

Stuck Down the Toilet

Jimmy was tough, Jimmy was bold,
The trouble is that Jimmy was one year old...

...when he said to himself *I look daft on this potty,*
There must be somewhere better for me to put my botty,
So he walked up the stairs and he checked out the loo,
When Jimmy was quite satisfied he said 'It'll do!'

Jimmy was tough, Jimmy was bold,
The trouble is that Jimmy was one year old.

He lifted up the cover and he sat himself down,
At first he was a-smiling but he soon began to frown,
His bottom wasn't wide enough, he fell in with a *PLOP*!
He'd only tried to sit down but he found he couldn't stop.

Jimmy was tough, Jimmy was bold,
The trouble is that Jimmy was one year old.

Jimmy couldn't get out so he yelled out for his sis'
Who, looking flabbergasted, chuckled 'How could you miss?'
She telephoned a doctor, he said 'Take it like a man,
I'm afraid to tell you Jimmy you must carry the can!'

Jimmy was tough, Jimmy was bold,
The trouble is that Jimmy was one year old.

Well, the doctor phoned the plumber and the plumber split his sides,
'If you're going to sit on toilets then your bottom should be wide,'
Then the plumber phoned a builder and the builder brought a hammer,
A bag like the doctor's and a very large spanner.

Jimmy was tough, Jimmy was bold,
The trouble is that Jimmy was one year old.

The builder got a rope and he tied it round Jim's tummy,
But Jimmy wasn't moving, he began to blubber 'Mummy,'
Mummy came a-running shouting 'Jimmy's down the loo!,'
Nothing could remove him, he was stuck like glue.

Jimmy was tough, Jimmy was bold,
The trouble is that Jimmy was one year old.

Then Jimmy had a cunning plan, he yelled 'Never fear!'
He strained for a minute and he blew himself clear,
So if you're about one year old or even slightly less,
Stick to your potty or you'll wind up in a mess!

Stuck Down the Toilet

Stuck Down the Toilet (one of the most popular items in my performance set!) is an example of a form with a repeating chorus which the class/group can join in with.

An activity which I develop from this is the 'slogan-hunt'. Over a period of time (usually a week) the pupils have to hunt for two-line rhyming slogans, both in the environment and in newspapers, magazines etc. These are added to a 'slogan collection board' and are used as the chorus between stanzas of poems which the pupils develop.

This provides a springboard into the study of persuasive writing techniques in the wider sense.

Key Objective:

To write poetry based on the structure and / or style of poems read, e.g. taking account of vocabulary, archaic expressions, patterns of rhyme, *choruses*, similes.

poem

'Dad, I've got a headache in my tummy...

...and it's growling like a lion with a sore paw,
rumbling like a washing machine on its last legs,
gurgling like water past a carrot in a plughole!'

'So *you* put the carrot in the bath,' said dad.
'Dad, I've got a headache in my tummy,' I replied.

Dad, I've got a headache in my tummy...

Dad I've got a headache in my tummy... can be employed to introduce the concept of *free verse* (unrhymed verse without a metrical pattern). Although there is no metrical pattern, free verse is often structured. One way of helping pupils to understand the difference between structured free verse and rhymed verse is to ban the use of rhyme and then to write a poem in three stanzas with the following opening lines:

> Dad, I've got a headache,
> Dad, my stomach's rumbling,
> Dad, I've got a sore foot,

Following each of these, the pupils have to give three reasons as to why they have a headache/rumbling stomach/sore foot. The resulting poem will be an example of structured free verse. (Note that in the example included in this collection three descriptions of what a 'headache in the tummy' sounds like are given – this could be extended and each trio of descriptions could be divided into separate stanzas.)

Another way of using the poem to explore structures is to focus on the last two lines and the use of dialogue in poetry. A humorous way to develop this is to suggest two types of characters such as:

1 A person who always asks questions.
2 A person who doesn't listen properly and answers in a way which doesn't make sense.

(There are innumerable variations on these character traits.)

Character one speaks the first line of the poem; character two continues with the second line; character one takes the third line and so forth so that the resulting poem might begin:

> What time is it?
> No you can't
> Is it half past ten yet?
> The hen is not wet!
> etc.

Key Objective:

To write poems, experimenting with different *styles and structures*. Discuss if and why different forms are more suitable than others.

poem

The Not-very-vegetarian Monster Chef's Treat!

I'd like to cook you something good,
A chocolate coated bat with mud,
A pie of feathers lightly baked,
A jellied stone, a candied snake,
A years-old egg, mouldy and rotten,
The kind of dish not soon forgotten,
A pair of wellies soaked in brine,
It makes me hungry, sounds divine.
But that will only be a start,
The main course? It's a work of art!

Arranged around a simple dish,
A dozen slugs, the eyes of fish,
All resting in a grey-green sauce
Of chopped-up, boiled old socks of course.
You'll wash it down with warmed-up sludge
Then finish with a seaweed fudge.
And after when you're all full up,
I'll bring to you a special cup
Of cat's hair coffee topped with froth
Which always nicely rounds things off!

The Not-very-vegetarian Monster Chef's Treat!

When using this poem in workshops with classes of children, I introduce it as a draft which I am not yet convinced is complete. I explain that there are some lines with which I am happy and others which I think can be improved. I then ask the class for their assistance and demonstrate a method I use to generate more ideas.

The 'polished poem method' has the following rules:

1. The rhyme scheme of the original poem must be retained
2. The overall meaning of the original poem must be retained
3. The entirety of each alternate line must be deleted
4. For each line deleted an entirely new alternative must be generated.

I then divide the class into two groups. Group one deletes lines 2/4/6/8, etc. and group two deletes lines 3/5/9, etc. They then produce alternatives for each deleted line. Line one is never altered as this usually helps the pupils to retain the overall meaning of the poem. (There is an opportunity to explore the use of rhyming dictionaries with the pupils in a purposeful manner during this activity.)

Next, a range of suggestions are read out for alternative 'line twos' by pupils in the first group and I choose an example to replace mine. It is important to demonstrate that all contributions are valued and it is worth explaining why one particular example has been chosen. If a fairly long poem is used to start with, then a large number of pupils' suggestions can be incorporated into the final 'polished' example. If two or three poems are used over a period of time, all children, even in a large class, will have helped to replace a line. This activity functions as a great motivator and teaches the pupils one method of revising/ redrafting which can be applied in their own writing.

If you try this activity with poems other than the example given, best results are achieved if you select a poem containing an element of listing. The use of separate ingredients on each of the lines of the example given helps the pupils to retain the meaning.

Key Objectives:

a) To produce polished poetry through revision, e.g. *deleting words, adding words, changing words*, reorganising words and lines, experimenting with figurative language.

b) To use a range of dictionaries and understand their purposes, e.g. dictionaries of slang, phrases, idioms, contemporary usage, synonyms, antonyms, quotations and thesauruses.

poem

The Register

(An Initials Poem!)

Nigel Barton: Naughty boy

Billy Beaumont: Bottom-biter

Alan Finch: Always fighting

Tina Louise Fisher: Two left feet

Colin King: Clever kid

Tony Sparks: Terrible speller

William Ian Tony Taylor: Whoops, I'm the teacher!

The Register

A form which never fails to excite 7-12 year olds is the 'initials poem'. In the example given, an imaginary register is taken, and after each person's name is called a description of that person, which uses the initials of their name, follows, e.g. Nigel Barton: naughty boy, etc.

Extensions include an alteration of the class register (with a ban on unkind descriptions!) and a famous people poem, e.g.

Alan Shearer: always scoring

In order to differentiate this activity, which is more complex than it at first seems, variations include 'animals' initials poems'. Here the animal's name is followed by either *words or phrases* beginning with the initial letter of the animal's name, which describe what the animal does, e.g.

*D*olphins *d*ive
*W*ombats *w*obble their tails

The most complex variation is the development of an initials poem which utilises the initials of the words in the title in each subsequent line. This is best explained by example:

Angry Teacher

Alphabet test
All terrible
Alice trembling
Albert tearful
Always tough -
Angry teacher!

Key Objective:

To write poems, experimenting with different styles and *structures*. Discuss if and why different forms are more suitable than others.

The Sleeping Snowman

In a morning in December when the sky was full of snow
And my nose was blue and freezing (it was ten
degrees below),
I came upon a snowman in a field behind my house,
I said 'Hello', but he stood still, as quiet as a mouse,
So I stepped a little closer but he didn't make a peep –
It was only then I worked it out... the snowman
was asleep!
Well I left him to his snoozing and I played out on my bike
Then I put my boots on quickly and I went out for a hike,
I quite forgot the snowman and I had a lot of fun
Until I woke next morning to a blue sky and a sun.
I went back to that snowman – the tears rolled down
his cheeks
And he cried himself to nothing, but I never heard
him speak.

The Sleeping Snowman

The Sleeping Snowman can be used to facilitate an awareness of the way that poetry conveys feelings and moods. After reading it, ask the simple question 'How did the poem make you feel?' This is followed by the more difficult question, 'Why?' Invariably the answer is, 'Because the snowman was crying/ sad/unhappy'. This presents the teacher with an opportunity to discuss hidden meanings in poems and, although this is a difficult concept for a 7–12 year-old to grasp, it is worth raising. A third question, 'Can a snowman really cry ?' is the key to this discussion. If you then ask, 'What was really happening to the snowman?' the answer that he was melting will be elicited. This could be followed by a discussion about how we project our feelings into/on to other objects in poetry.

Choose an object, e.g. a plant. The class then project an emotion on to the plant. If they choose *sadness*, a useful first line would be:

> Still and silent, brown leaves fall from it.

This could then be developed as a group before individual pupils choose their own object and attach an emotion to it.

A phrase that is worth sharing with pupils is 'show not tell'. It is more effective for a poet to show us that a person is sad rather than to tell us. For example,

> With drooping shoulders and head hanging down he walked (show)

is more effective than

> The sad man walked (tell)

An additional area of discussion is the way that writers use weather to convey a mood. The phrase,'bright, sunny day', creates one kind of mood whereas 'stormy, cloudy night', creates a very different one. Phrases which include reference to the weather could then be attached to different mood-words such as sadness/fear/happiness.

Key Objective:

To convey feelings, reflections or moods in a poem through the careful choice of words and phrases.

The World's Worst Vampire

The first time that I met him he was bathing in the sun,
Splashing suntan lotion on and saying, 'This is fun!'
'You're not supposed to like it Vlad, lying in the light,
You're meant to shrivel in the sun and come out when it's night.'

I thought, 'He needs tuition, he's the worst vampire I've seen,'
I told him to stop smiling and start by acting mean,
Round his neck he wore a crucifix, he'd got it from his mum,
I even caught him loading silver bullets in his gun.

He needed serious talking to, I took him for a meal,
He filed his fangs down for it, said it gave him fresh appeal.
The waiter took his order, 'Yes, I'll have a steak,' he cried,
'How d'you like it?', 'Sharp and wooden,'...well the waiter
merely sighed.

He walked off mumbling, '*Joker*,' but Vlad just didn't care,
The steak arrived soon after and he noticed it was rare,
He screamed and then he fainted, he was frightened by the blood,
In terms of basic *Vampireness* he really was no good.

He came round screaming 'Garlic!', we brought some, he felt better,
If you've met a Vamp who's daft and wet, believe me, Vlad is wetter.
He's afraid of horror movies, says that musicals are best,
Likes to wander round his castle wearing Y-fronts and a vest.

His favourite food is lettuce and a dainty bunch of grapes,
If you shout out, '**BOO!**' at Vlad he'll simply tremble in his cape,
He won't sleep in his coffin, says 'It really cramps my style,'
He's always kind and quite polite but should be acting vile.

I helped out with his problem but I simply got fatigue,
As a scary, evil vampire, Vlad comes bottom of the league.

The World's Worst Vampire

The following is a practical method of teaching the concept of metaphor to 7-12 year olds.

After reading *The World's Worst Vampire* divide a large sheet of paper into three columns. Then label the two columns to the right with the titles:

Bad people or creatures from books and films
Good people or creatures from books and films

In the column on the left list the following headings:

Time of day/Weather/Car/Place/Food/Hobby

The page should appear as follows:

	Bad people or...	Good people or...
Time of day		
Weather		
Car		
Place		
Food		
Hobby		

Now ask the pupils to suggest a bad and good person or creature from a book or film and write their suggestions at the top of the table.

Then ask them to suggest a bad time of day and a good time of day and write these in the appropriate spaces. I often find it best to model the first two answers, e.g. bad time of day: six a.m. when the alarm goes off; good time of day: midday when I have my dinner.

If Dracula and Snow White had been suggested as characters, our first two columns when put together would read:

Dracula is six a.m. when the alarm goes off.
Snow White is midday when I have my dinner.

Hey presto! Two metaphors! The process is repeated for each of the other columns thereby creating a large number of metaphors. It can then be explained that a metaphor describes something as something else – a very difficult concept made concrete with this exercise.

Key Objective:

To write metaphors from original ideas or from similes.

poem

Mary had a little...lion

Mary had a little lion,
She liked him, she called him *Brian*
Everywhere that Mary walked
Her lion, Brian, also stalked,
Until one day he licked his lips,
But didn't fancy fish and chips
And so he ate his owner Mary,
Who, for a while, felt quite contrary,
Her last words, 'Help me, oh I am
A girl who wished she'd bought a lamb.'

Mary had a little... lion

Mary had a little... lion is an example of an altered nursery rhyme and as such is a variation on an existing structure. There are many ways in which existing nursery rhymes can be varied: additional verses can be created by substituting different kinds of animals at the end of the first line, e.g. *Mary had a little cat.*

When modelling an example with the class/group it is important to ask for a range of suggested rhyming words for the second line, i.e. hat/sat/that/bat, etc. Following this a range of 'possible' second lines can be produced, such as,

> Mary had a little cat,
> A donkey, lion and fruit bat,
> etc.

When a broad range have been produced, the pupils can be asked to choose a favourite second line and discuss why they have chosen it. A point to consider in this discussion is the avoidance of forced rhymes (a dog/on a log/in a bog!).

You can then further discuss how certain of the second lines suggest extensions. In the example given above, a logical development would be for Mary to open her own zoo. By discussing this explicitly the teacher is demonstrating how the first two lines can be developed so that the poem 'works' as a unified idea rather than as a disjointed sequence of rhyming couplets.

An additional method of adding further verses is to ask for verbs which could be used to end the first line, such as:

> Mary had a little sleep/run/walk/fall

and then to *expand the idea* – a process which should be modelled by the teacher. If, for example, we choose 'Mary had a little sleep', the idea could be expanded so that she...

(a) sleeps for a thousand years
(b) sleeps until someone/thing woke her up with a kiss!
(c) sleeps through the worst storm ever

Pupils can suggest other *expansions.*

An activity which helps pupils to structure their poetry is 'Questions of the First Line'. To do this, the first line is written down and then ten questions are asked of it. If the first line is 'Mary had a little sleep', questions could include: 'how long did she sleep?'; 'where was she sleeping?'; 'what made her sleep?', etc.

The pupils then have to answer as many of these questions as they can when writing their poem.

Key Objective:

To use the structures of poems read to write extensions based on these, e.g. additional verses, or substituting own words and ideas.

poem

You'd Better Beware (A Reptile Rap)

Colin McNaughton

You'd better beware, if you come round here,
To watch your step, to steer well clear
Of my front gate, it's a dangerous place
Because you might come face to face
With my new pet, who's big and mean,
The ugliest brute you've ever seen.

Crooks and robbers don't come near,
They creep right past, they shake with fear.
They'd rather spend a year in gaol
Than risk one tickle from his fingernail.
Claws like razors, teeth like knives,
They'd better get lost, better run for their lives.

So if you're broke or out of work,
Get pushed around and called a jerk,
And if you're sad or if you're blue,
Take my advice, this is what you do:
Go down to the monster store
And get yourself a dinosaur.

Beat that drum, bang that gong,
Six metres high by sixteen long,
Come on all join in the chorus
My new pet's a Tyrannosaurus!

You'd Better Beware (A Reptile Rap) (Colin McNaughton)

A 'rap' is basically the modern equivalent of a ballad in that it retains a strong narrative element. The two differ because a ballad usually contains a recurrent refrain whereas a rap generally does not.

Most raps are formed using rhyming couplets and are ideal to use for performance as they are 'rapped' in 4/4 time with an accent on the first 'beat-word' of the bar.

After performing the included example, pupils can write their own raps. Useful starting lines include:

(a) Hi, I'm an alien from outer space
(b) I was out in the street when I had a surprise
(c) A long time ago in a place far away

In workshops I usually develop 'Hi, I'm an alien from outer space' with the whole class/group prior to letting them develop examples (b) and (c). I do this because (a) is content-specific whereas (b) and (c) are open-ended. In a workshop I use example (a) and focus on the rhyming word at the end of the line before asking the class/group to suggest other words that could form a couplet with this in the second line, e.g. face/suitcase, etc. I then model a second line using one of the suggestions, e.g.

I've got twenty-five legs and a really weird face.

Following this, we work on lines three and four by (at first) disregarding rhyme and concentrating on what might happen next. This helps to ensure that the focus is firmly placed upon meaning rather than rhyming. We then develop a third line (remembering that it doesn't rhyme with lines one and two) and then return to the process of rhyming word suggestion as we did with line two. This joint approach helps the pupils to understand the dynamics of the form.

Key Objective:

To use performance poems as models to write and to produce poetry in polished forms through revising, redrafting and presentation.

poem

My Life as a Pencil!

The zip moved and light flooded in!
I'd been lying in that case for days,
Not a soul to speak to, not a thing to do;
Boy was it good to see the sun again...
...and then she picked me up and held me
and for a moment I was filled with a joy that warmed me
right down to my lead –
I've learned that moments like this never last.

The nightmare began as she turned me upside down,
Pressed my head hard against the paper
And, horror of horrors, just scribbled away,
Nothing productive, nothing useful,
Just doodling and drawing as I gradually grew flatter –
I knew that soon I'd be taken to that dreadful place,
The thing all pencils fear...
...the sharpener!

Well, as sure as day is day,
She spun my head around inside it,
Shaved me down to the finest of points
Stripped me of my wooden coat,
But as I grew sharper I also grew shorter –
You know how it is; a short pencil won't last long.
My days are numbered, this could be the last time we speak,
I live in fear of that final resting place –
The bin!

My Life as a Pencil

My Life as a Pencil can be used when introducing the concept of personification which, strictly, is the attribution of human characteristics to non-human things. 'Bringing something to life which has never lived before' tends to help 7–12 year-olds to understand the concept.

To develop a further understanding of the concept, try the following activity.

Activity: Bring an object to life

Choose an object in the classroom and complete the following writing frame as if the object itself is speaking

I like...

I don't like...

I'm afraid of...

I am happy when...

________________ makes me sad

I'd rather be ________________ because ________________

This exercise is useful as it reinforces the use of the first person pronoun and helps to develop empathy. The ability to assume an alternative frame of reference is one of the tools in an effective poet's armoury.

The above activity can also be applied to two entirely different objects in order to deepen the pupils' understanding of personification.

Key Objective:

To write own poems experimenting with active verbs and *personification*; produce *revised poems* for reading aloud individually.

poem

Spike!

He's a hedgehog with a difference, you've never seen the like,
Wait there for a moment while I introduce 'Spike',
You shouldn't feel terrified, you shouldn't feel glum,
Stroke his nose gently and he'll always be your chum.
OK, so he's bigger than a lorry or a bus,
OK, so he's a giant, so tell me 'What's the fuss?',
He's beaten BMWs, he's fought off Ford Fiestas,
He's fearlessly crossed the road in London, Leeds and Leicester.
He's taken on our motorways, he laughs at country lanes,
He's a legend among hedgehogs, come sun or hail or rain.
Tales are told at dead of night of things that Spike has done,
Wars with overloaded trucks that Spike has rightly won.
He'll puncture cross-ply radials, he'll split your tyres' rubber,
When lorry drivers spot him they will often start to blubber.
Cars swerve to avoid him and drivers yell out 'Gosh!',
Other hedgehogs come and go but Spike will never squash.

Spike!

Spike! tells the tale of a giant hedgehog which attacks motorists! The idea of expanding or contracting the size of a creature could be developed as a feature of the form of the poem itself. If the poem is based on the theme of a creature growing in size then the structure of the poem itself could mirror this so that the first line is one word long, the second line is two words long, the third line three words, and so on.

When teaching this 'expanding' poem format it is best to explain that each line should encompass an entire idea otherwise the 'poem' is merely segmented prose.

An example for classroom use which relates to the poem *Spike!* follows :

Spike!
He's huge!
A giant hedgehog!
Drivers must watch out.
He is fearless and strong,
etc.

(Pupils could 'finish' this example as a group before working individually or in pairs on their own poems.)

Variations on this theme are numerous. We can change the animal: what would happen if an ant grew to an enormous size?, etc. We can also focus on an emotion: what if someone's anger grew and grew?

An alternative is to write a contracting poem in which a large animal, such as an elephant, shrinks. The first line (which is between 10 and 15 words long) reduces in length by one word on each subsequent line. The initial two lines could, therefore, read:

Mike was a happy and content elephant of quite large proportions
(11 words)
Until that day when he knew that he was shrinking
(10 words)

Note: A contracting poem is more difficult to produce than an expanding poem.

After producing a range of both expanding and contracting poems linked by theme (as suggested) the pupils can collect them in their own anthology.

Key Objective:

To write a sequence of poems linked by a theme or form, e.g. a haiku calendar.

poem

Fishy Tale

Colin McNaughton

My friend Brian says
that all the people who live in Finland
have fins because they eat so much fish.
My Dad says it's not true
but I think it might be.

Fishy Tale (Colin McNaughton)

Whilst I have attached this activity suggestion to *Fishy Tale*, it actually relates to a number of the poems in this volume. It involves the pupils in the writing of a summary of either part or the whole of this book and, although it does not involve them in writing a poem, the critical appraisal of other writers' poetry undoubtedly helps to shape their work.

It is important that this summary; which can be introduced as a 'book review', should not be a mere retell. In order to avoid the pitfall of retell you need to provide guidelines and explore modelled examples of reviews. Useful sentence starters can be extracted and a 'phrasebank' should be produced. (This can be cumulative rather than 'fixed', i.e. there should be sufficient space for it to be expanded later if it is used as a visual referent.)

My personal guidelines for reviewing, which I share with the pupils, are as follows:

1 The review should describe the forms utilised by the poet.

2 The review should include comments about the poet's style and use of language.

3 Short extracts from poems should be used as examples in the review.

4 The reviewer should always have a target audience in mind. (You can specify this prior to writing.)

5 The review should include personal preferences – the reviewer must state *why* they prefer some poems to others.

6 The review should include a summary which states for whom the book/excerpt is suitable.

These guidelines are not immutable but are specific to reviews of poetry.

Key Objective:

To write summaries of books or parts of books, deciding on priorities relevant to purpose.

poem

Haiku for a Hot Snowman

Oh no! It's the sun,
I'm not ready for meltdown...
There goes my carrot!

Haiku for a Hot Snowman

After reading this poem, explain that a haiku is a 17-syllable Japanese poetic form arranged as follows:

Line 1 : 5 syllables
Line 2 : 7 syllables
Line 3 : 5 syllables

The example given is humorous although the haiku is not primarily a humorous form. For a more serious approach it is worth explaining that a haiku should capture a moment in time and perhaps 'see' something in that moment that no-one else will see.

This seven-syllable middle line from a haiku about a storm better explains what I am driving at:

Houses shake in the puddles

Once the basics of the form have been understood, it is possible to write a haiku sequence (known as a 'renga'). To do this the pupils need to understand that in traditional haiku sequences, the collection was ordered according to the seasons, and that each haiku in the collection included a season-word or phrase known as a 'kigo'.

A Spring kigo could be 'new born lambs'
An Autumn kigo, 'brown leaves'
A Winter kigo, 'frosty ground'

A completed haiku about winter for the haiku-sequence (renga) might read...

It's dark so early,
Under streetlight frosty ground
Glitters like diamonds.

The kigo 'frosty ground' has been included and the poem would be collected in the 'Winter' section of the renga.

An extension activity is the writing of 'tanka', another Japanese syllabic form, 5 lines in length with the following syllabic pattern:

5 / 7 / 5 / 7 / 7 syllables

Further information about Haiku writing can be found under 'Free resources' at www.alanpeat.com

Key Objective:

To write a sequence of poems linked by a theme or *form*, e.g. a haiku calendar.